MEAN FREE PATH

BOOKS BY BEN LERNER

Mean Free Path

Angle of Yaw

The Lichtenberg Figures

MEAN FREE PATH

BEN LERNER

COPPER CANYON PRESS

PORT TOWNSEND, WASHINGTON

Cover art: A long-exposure photograph of U.S. Peacekeeper III reentry vehicles splashing down during a test near the Kwajalein Atoll in the Republic of the Marshall Islands. Image courtesy of the United States Army.

Copper Canyon Press is in residence at Fort Worden State Park in Port Townsend, Washington, under the auspices of Centrum. Centrum is a gathering place for artists and creative thinkers from around the world, students of all ages and backgrounds, and audiences seeking extraordinary cultural enrichment.

LIBRARY OF CONGRESS CATALOGING-IN-PUBLICATION DATA
Lerner, Ben, 1979-
 Mean free path / Ben Lerner.
    p. cm.
 ISBN 978-1-55659-314-7 (pbk. : alk. paper)
 I. Title.
 PS3612.E68M43 2010
 811'.6—dc22

                          2009043652

COPPER CANYON PRESS
Post Office Box 271
Port Townsend, Washington 98368
www.coppercanyonpress.org

ACKNOWLEDGMENTS

Grateful acknowledgment is made to *Critical Quarterly* (UK), *Jacket, jubilat, Lana Turner, Narrative, The Nation, New American Writing, The New Review of Literature, The Paris Review, A Public Space,* and *The Seattle Review,* where some of these poems first appeared.

I would like to thank Geoffrey, Cyrus, Ed, and my parents for their attention to these poems.

MEAN FREE PATH

DEDICATION

For the distances collapsed.
         For the figure
failed to humanize
the scale. For the work,
the work did nothing but invite us
to relate it to
         the wall.
For I was a shopper in a dark
         aisle.

For the mode of address
         equal to the war
was silence, but we went on
celebrating doubleness.
For the city was polluted
with light, and the world,
         warming.
For I was a fraud
         in a field of poppies.

For the rain made little
         affective adjustments
to the architecture.
For the architecture was a long
lecture lost on me, negative
mnemonics reflecting
         weather
and reflecting
         reflecting.

For I felt nothing,
        which was cool,
totally cool with me.
For my blood was cola.
For my authority was small
involuntary muscles
        in my face.
For I had had some work done
        on my face.

For I was afraid
        to turn
left at intersections.
For I was in a turning lane.
For I was signaling,
despite myself,
        the will to change.
For I could not throw my voice
        away.

For I had overslept,
        for I had dressed
in layers for the long
dream ahead, the recurring
dream of waking with
alternate endings
        she'd walk me through.
For Ariana.

        For Ari.

MEAN FREE PATH

I finished the reading and looked up
Changed in the familiar ways. Now for a quiet place
To begin the forgetting. The little delays
Between sensations, the audible absence of rain
Take the place of objects. I have some questions
But they can wait. Waiting is the answer
I was looking for. Any subject will do
So long as it recedes. Hearing the echo
Of your own blood in the shell but picturing
The ocean is what I meant by

$$\propto$$

You startled me. I thought you were sleeping
In the traditional sense. I like looking
At anything under glass, especially
Glass. *You* called *me*. Like overheard
Dreams. I'm writing this one as a woman
Comfortable with failure. I promise I will never
But the predicate withered. If you are
Uncomfortable seeing this as portraiture
Close your eyes. No, *you* startled

Identical cities. How sad. Buy up the run
The unsigned copies are more valuable
I have read your essay about the new
Closure. My favorite parts I cannot follow
Surface effects. We moved to Canada
Without our knowledge. If it reciprocates the gaze
How is it pornography? Definitions crossed
With stars, the old closure, which reminds me
Wave to the cameras from the

$$\propto$$

The petals are glass. That's all you need to know
Lines have been cut and replaced
With their opposites. Did I say that out loud
A beautiful question. Barbara is dead
Until I was seventeen, I thought windmills
Turned from the fireworks to watch
Their reflection in the tower
Made wind. Brushed metal apples
Green to the touch

All pleads for an astounding irrelevance
Structured like a language, but I
I like the old music, the audible kind
We made love to in the crawl space
Without our knowledge. Robert is dead
Take my voice. I don't need it. Take my face
I have others. Pathos whistles through the typos
Parentheses slam shut. I'm writing this one
With my eyes closed, listening to the absence of

$$\propto$$

Surface effects. Patterns of disappearance. I
I kind of lost it back there in the trees, screaming
About the complexity of intention, but
But nothing. Come to bed. Reference is a woman
Comfortable with failure. The surface is dead
Wave to the cameras from the towers
Built to sway. I promised I would never
Tell me, whose hand is this. A beautiful
Question her sources again

Unhinged in a manner of speaking
Crossed with stars, a rain that can be paused
So we know we're dreaming on our feet
Like horses in the city. How sad. Maybe
No maybes. Take a position. Don't call it
Night-vision green. Think of the children
Running with scissors through the long
Where were we? If seeing this as portraiture
Makes you uncomfortable, wake up

∝

Wake up, it's time to begin
The forgetting. Direct modal statements
Wither under glass. A little book for Ari
Built to sway. I admire the use of felt
Theory, like swimming in a storm, but object
To antirepresentational bias in an era of
You're not listening. I'm sorry. I was thinking
How the beauty of your singing reinscribes
The hope whose death it announces. Wave

In an unconscious effort to unify my voice
I swallow gum. An old man weeps in the airport
Over a missed connection. The color of money is
Night-vision green. Ari removes the bobby pins
I remove the punctuation. Our freezer is empty
Save for vodka and film. Leave the beautiful
Questions unanswered. There are six pages left
Of our youth and I would rather swallow my tongue
Than waste them on description

∝

A cry goes up for plain language
In identical cities. Zukofsky appears in my dreams
Selling knives. Each exhibit is a failed futurity
A star survived by its own light. Glass anthers
Confuse bees. Is that pornography? Yes, but
But nothing. Come to reference. A mode of undress
Equal to fascism becomes obligatory
In identical cities. Did I say that already? Did I say
The stranglehold of perspective must be shaken off

A live tradition broadcast with a little delay
Takes the place of experience, like portraits
Reciprocating gazes. Zukofsky appears in my dreams
Offering his face. Each of us must ask herself
Why am I clapping? The content is announced
Through disappearance, like fireworks. Wave
After wave of information breaks over us
Without our knowledge. If I give you my denim
Will you simulate distress

$$\propto$$

To lay everything waste in the name of renewal
Haven't we tried that before? Yes, but
But not in Canada. The vanguard succumbs
To a sense of its own importance as easily as swans
Succumb to the flu. I'm writing this one
With my nondominant hand in the crawl space
Under the war. I can feel an axis snapping
In my skull, and soon I will lose the power
To select, while retaining the power to

All these flowers look the same to me
Night-vision green. There is nothing to do
In the desert but read *Penthouse* and lift weights
My blood is negative. That's all you need to know
Sophisticated weaponry marries the traditional
Pleasures of perspective to the new materiality
Of point-and-click. I'm writing this one
As a woman comfortable with leading
A prisoner on a leash

∝

Combine was the word I was looking for
Back there in the trees. My blood is
Scandinavian Modern. I kind of lost it
But enough about me. To return with a difference
Haven't we tried that before? Yes, but
But not from the air. Unique flakes form
Indistinguishable drifts in a process we call
All these words look the same to me
Fascism. Arrange the flowers by their price

Then, where despair had been, the voice
Of Nina Simone. Parentheses open
On a new gender crossed with stars
Ari removes the bobby pins. Night falls
There is no such thing as non sequitur
When you're in love. Let those who object
To the pathos swallow their tongues. My numb
Rebarbative people, put down your Glocks
And your Big Gulps. We have birthmarks to earn

$$\propto$$

Around 1945 the question becomes: Sleepyhead
Since the world is ending, may I eat the candy
Necklace off your body? Turn the record over
Turn the pillow over. It has a cooler side
Like a vein on the wing of a locust
The seam of hope disclosed by her voice
It cannot save us. But it can remind us
Survival is a butcher's goal. All hands
To the pathos. Let the credits

Bend the plastic stick and break the interior tube
The reaction emits light, but not heat
The tragedy of dialectics. Sand-sized particles
Of revolutionary possibility fall constantly
Without our knowledge. The capitol lawns
Sparkle with poison. Since the world is ending
Why not let the children touch the paintings
The voice of Nina Simone contains its own
Negation, like a pearl

∝

As brand names drift toward the generic
We drift toward fascism, a life in common
Replaced with its image. The predicates
Are glass. I blew them. I'm sorry, sorrier
Than I can say on such a tiny phone. You're
Breaking up. No, down. I held the hand
Of a complete stranger during takeoff
Unaware it was my own, laying bare
The ideological function of

Numbness, felt silence, a sudden
Inability to swallow, the dream in which
The face is Velcro, describing the film
In the language of disaster, the disaster in
Not finishing sentences, removing the suicide
From the speed dial, failing to recognize
Yourself in the photo, coming home to find
A circle of concerned family and friends
It's more of an artists' colony than a hospital

$\propto$

It's more of a vitamin than an antipsychotic
Collective despair expressed in I-statements
The dream in which the skin is stonewashed
Denim, running your hand through the hair
Of an imaginary friend, rising from bed
Dressing, returning calls, all without
Waking, the sudden suspicion the teeth
In your mouth are not your own, let
Alone the words

She handed me a book. I had read it before
Dismissed it, but now, in the dark, I heard
The little delays. If you would speak of love
Stutter, like rain, like Robert, be
Be unashamed. Let those who object to the
But that's familiar rage. It isn't a system
It is a gesture whose power derives from its
Failure, a child attempting to gather
Us into her glitter-flecked arms

∝

It isn't a culture of fear. When a people
Pats itself on the back with a numb hand
It isn't a culture at all. Take a position
Cut it off. Leave the rings. The president
But you promised you wouldn't mention
I saw myself in the mirrored lenses
You cannot kill a metonym
Of his bodyguards. I'm moving to Canada
When I wake up. You mean *if*

No concept of clockwise rotation can be
Described on the surface continuously
So this might take a while. Bring a book
Have you tried breaking it into triangles
Or changing hands. No, handedness
Fascia, a tangent bundle. Can we unfold
What we can't figure? Not without making
Cuts. Orient me, for the night is coming
Amphichiral, manifold, and looped

$$\propto$$

We have no reason to hope, but what's reason
What's reason got to do with it? Accent
Not duration. Cantillation, not punctuation
And that's love. Why not speak of it
As we are drawn up into the rising
Toroidal fireball? This column
Of powdery light is made possible
By Boeing, but what, and here's where people
Start disappearing, made Boeing possible

If you could see the tip of the vector
It would appear to be moving in a circle
As it approached you. Reference is a slow
Wave transporting energy through empty
Media. You can't rush it. The displaced
Pathos returns with a vengeance and painters
Pull grids apart in grief. Only a master
Only a butcher can unmake sense. The rest of us
Have axes to grind into glass

$\propto$

By *complex* I mean my intention is drawn
Downward to the bottom of the cloud
It hurts me when you listen too closely
Smothering reference. Carefully decanted
Left to breathe. *That's* criticism. The subject
Rises to the surface. Bursts. All light paths
From the object to the image are reversible
And that hurts, to know it didn't have to be
I mean, don't get me wrong, I enjoy killing

Birds were these little ships that flew and sang
There are some cool pics online. Funny
Strange, not ha-ha funny, how the black
Canvas grows realistic, a bird's-eye view
Of their disappearance. Wave after wave
Of déjà lu. After the storm, the sky turns
Night-vision green. The color of murder
I can hear the soldiers marching in my
Pillow. Even in Canada

$$\propto$$

Her literature is irrelevant to October
Anna of all the Russias, whose body was
An ideal October that has yet to obtain
A face. October approached asymptotically
By tanks. The leaves turn night-vision
Anna, do you see how the sand-sized particles
Of the true October rise from the asphalt
Like fireflies whose bodies are night-vision
Neither do I. The irrelevant I. The I of all

It will develop recursively or not at all
The new closure. In lieu of fixed outlines
Modulating color. If concentrated light
Strikes the leaf, part is reflected through
The droplet, producing a white glow around
The genre. It's like the whispering gallery
The fighter pilot sees his shadow on the cloud
Crossed with the Wailing Wall. We can't
Distinguish rounds of ammunition from

$$\propto$$

Applause. Speak plainly. Keep your hands
On the table. Do not flee into procedure
Do not wait for a surpassing disaster
To look your brother in the eye and speak
Of love. Make no mistake: the disjunction
The disjunction stays. Do not hesitate
To cut the most beautiful line in the name
Of form. The bread of words. Look for me
At genre's edge. I'm going there on foot

I dyed what's-her-face's hair with lime
Kool-Aid so when I read "Bezhin Meadow"
I lent her aspect to the green-haired spirit
There is a girl trapped in every manmade lake
She will pull you into your reflection
Stephen tells me what's-her-face
Who used to sleepwalk into the snow
Piss her name and glide back to bed
Without waking was thrown

$$\propto$$

Into this poem through a windshield
Once she gathered me into her glitter-flecked
I don't care if "aspect" is archaic
Once she walked into the sliding door
A plane announced through disappearance
You made it this far without mentioning
Topeka. Glass in her hair. Patterns of
I will throw my voice like a clay pot
Keep her ashes there. I don't care if "love

I don't deny the influence, but it's less
A relation of father to son than a relation of
Moon to tide. Plus, my teachers are mainly
Particles bombarding gold foil or driving rain
It's the motion, not the material, not the nouns
But the little delays. A gender crossed
A genre crossed on foot by Marvin Gaye
Filicide. Strong misreadings arise
On the surface. Burst. It didn't have to be

$$\propto$$

If I rise from table, if I wander
Discalced through the sparkling lawns
If I'm lost in Juárez in Topeka, if it's winter
In August when the prodromata, when the birds
Cite the past in all its moments, there is no
No need for examples, police, doctors
Let me walk to the edge of the genre and look out
Into nothing. I will return, the fit will return me
In time for coffee and oranges

Authority derived from giving it away
Is how I define *aura,* like Zukofsky's
Paper flowers picked from *Kapital*
For Celia's hair. Priceless. The high
Reflective ceilings allow us to receive
Our own applause. When an audience
Takes a bow, that's fascism. A looped
Encore. Surface effects. The auditorium
Is a standing wave. A sedimented roar

∝

The entire system weighs about two pounds
A small bird governs the atria. You dream
The donor's dreams. The donor's breath
Breaks your lines across their prepositions
Halved and polished to display the crystal
Back-formations. Go in fear of abstraction
But go. Be gone by morning. There is nothing
You don't need a shell. Just cup your hand
Nothing for you here but repetition

DOPPLER ELEGIES

∝

By any measure, it was endless
           winter. Emulsions with
Then circled the lake like
This is it. This April will be
Inadequate sensitivity to green. I rose
early, erased for an hour
           Silk-brush and ax
I'd like to think I'm a different person
           latent image fading

around the edges and ears
           Overall a tighter face
now. Is it so hard for you to understand
From the drop-down menu
In a cluster of eight poems, I selected
sleep, but could not
           I decided to change everything
Composed entirely of stills
           or fade into the trees

but could not
           remember the dream
save for one brief shot
of a woman opening her eyes
Ari, pick up. I'm a different person
In a perfect world, this would be
           April, or an associated concept
Green to the touch
           several feet away

∝

I want to finish the book in time
            period. Confused bees
In a perfect world
a willow-effect. Rain on the recording
Fine with this particular form
of late everything, a spherical
            break of colored stars
a voice described as torn in places
            Why am I always

asleep in your poems
            Soft static falling through
The life we've chosen
from a drop-down menu
of available drives. Look at me
Ben, when am I
            This isn't my voice
At such-and-such smooth rate, the lines
            Stream at night

and love. Why not speak of it
            as all work now
is late work. Leafage, fountain, cloud
into whose sunlit depths
I'm quoting. Is there a place for this
she cut her hair
            She held it toward me
In your long dream
            money changes hands

∝

I'm worried about a friend
          among panicles of spent
flowers. I'm on the phone
There's an argument here regarding
Cathedral windows thicker at the base
It does not concern you
          flowing glass. Can we talk
about the drinking
          They call them smoke trees

I'm pretty much dead
          by any measure
already. When we were kids, the leaves
but that's a story, fallen or reflected
obscured the well. I cut this
In the dream, they are always
          younger. Ari woke me
You were screaming
          Everything is so

easy for you
          You mean was
so easy, like walking slowly
Out of the photo, even those
They are blooming early. I mean that
literally. You can see it from space
          he took. Can we talk
about the drinking
          Sometime in May

∝

The passengers are asked to clap
      It was always the same
window in his poems
for the two soldiers. We were delayed
In every seat, a tiny screen
A tiny bottle. The same traffic
      High up in the trees, small
rain. He held the subject
      constant. Now I

get it. I looked out
      over Denver, but could see
only our reflection. Dim
the cabin lights. Robert is dead
Articles may have shifted
I didn't know him. Why am I
      clapping. We are beginning
our final descent into
      A voice described as torn

On the recording, I could hear
      the hesitation
A certain courage. I can't explain
as music. We could watch
our own plane crash. We would be
Our men and women
      permitted to call down
in uniform. When I heard him live
      it was lost on me

∝

A flowering no one attends
          The enterprise known
variously as waking, April, or
Bats are disappearing like
color into function. I wanted to open
In a new window
          the eyes of a friend
by force if necessary. Amber light
          is a useless phrase

but will have to do
          what painting did
Dense smoke from the burning wells
for our parents. Ben
there is a man at the door who says
I've made small changes
          he found your notebook
throughout in red. The recurring dream
          contrived in places

Of waning significance
          it resembles the hand
after a difficult passage
opening, a key word in the early
Blue of rippled glass
atonal circles. They phased us out
          across the backward capitals
like paper money
          Or is that two words

∝

They are passing quickly, those
                    houses I wanted to
speak in. Empty sets
Among my friends, there is a fight about
The important questions
cannot arise, so those must be hills
                    where the famous
winter. I am familiar with the dream
                    Windmills enlarge

experience, killing birds
                    but I have already used
dream too often in my book
of relevance. Nothing can be predicated
Along the vanishing coast
tonight. You'll have to wait until
                    remnants of small fires
the eye can pull new features from
                    The stars

eat here. There is a private room
                    Are you concerned
about foreign energy
In your work, I sense a certain
distance, like a radio left on
Across the water, you can see
                    the new construction going up
is glass. The electric cars
                    unmanned

∝

Somewhere in this book I broke
       There is a passage
with a friend. I regret it now
lifted verbatim from
Then began again, my focus on
moving the lips, failures in
       The fuselage glows red against
rinsed skies. Rehearsing sleep
       I think of him from time

in a competitive field
       facedown, a familiar scene
composed entirely of stills
to time. It's hard to believe
When he calls, I pretend
he's gone. He was letting himself go
       I'm on the other line
in a cluster of eight poems
       all winter. The tenses disagreed

for Ari. Sorry if I've seemed
       distant, it's been a difficult
period, striking as many keys
with the flat of the hand
as possible, then leaning the head
against the window, unable to recall
       April, like overheard speech
at the time of writing
       soaked into its length

∝

Is this what you meant by prose
      Silica glass shapes
A supporting beam
where lightning strikes the sand
missing from the voice, eaten away
From the inside I could see
      his influence, mainly in the use
but also in exchange
      The head tipped back

to slow the speaking
      Our collaboration ends
On the appointed day, we gathered
in a makeshift structure
Viscous fluid from a floral source
but quarreled over terms
      pouring from the mouth into
Particles of wax. It's been done before
      cupped hands

in a lesser key, a broader sense
      I sound like him
more often now, unable to pronounce
or trailing off, then suddenly
Set against a large expanse
I have to leave. I just remembered
      something about Ari
structured like a language
      with appropriate delays

MEAN FREE PATH

What if I made you hear this as music
But not how you mean that. The slow beam
Opened me up. Walls walked through me
Like resonant waves. I thought that maybe
If you aren't too busy, we could spend our lives
Parting in stations, promising to write
War and Peace, this time with feeling
As bullets leave their luminous traces across
Wait, I wasn't finished. I was going to say
Breakwaters echo long lines of cloud

$$\propto$$

Renunciation scales. Exhibits shade
Imperceptibly into gift shops. The death of a friend
Opens me up. Suddenly the weather
Is written by Tolstoy, whose hands were giant
Resonant waves. It's hard not to take
When your eye is at the vertex of a cone
Autumn personally. My past becomes
Of lines extending to each leaf
Citable in all its moments: parting, rain

There must be an easier way to do this
I mean without writing, without echoes
Arising from focusing surfaces, which should
Should have been broken by structures
Hung from the apex in the hope of deflecting
In the hope of hearing the deflection of music
As music. There must be a way to speak
At a canted angle of enabling failures
The little collisions, the path of decay

$$\propto$$

But before it was used by the blind, it was used
By soldiers who couldn't light their lamps
Without drawing fire from across the lake
Embossed symbols enable us to read
Our orders silently in total dark
In total war, the front is continuous
Night writing, from which descends
Night-vision green. What if I made you
Hear this with your hands

Autumn in a minor novel. The school
Scatters, scattering light across the surface
Reforms around the ankle of the child
That you were. The end. Put the book away
Look out the window: we are descending
Like Chopin through the dusk. Now it's six
Six years later and I'm reading it again
Over Denver. I bought it in the gift shop
Nothing's changed except the key

∝

Little contrasts flicker in
Distances complex because collapsing
Under their own weight like stars
Embossed symbols. I can't compete
It's like the moment after waking
When you cannot determine if the screaming
With devices designed to amplify
Was internal or external to the dream
Starlight so soldiers can read in their sleep

Wait, I don't want this to turn
Turn into a major novel. I want this to be
Composed entirely of edges, a little path
For Ari. All my teachers have been women
But not how you mean that. That's why I speak
In a voice so soft it sounds like writing
Night writing. A structure of feeling
Broken by hand. I want the paper to have poor
Opacity, the verso just visible beneath

∝

The ode just visible beneath the elegy
The preemptive elegy composed entirely
This movement from the ground to cloud
Of waves decaying slowly on plucked strings
Is lightning. I don't know how else to say it
I mean without writing. Maybe if you let
The false starts stand, stand in for symbols
Near collapse, or let collapsing symbolize
The little clearing loving is. Maybe then

Stamp the interference pattern into green foil
Tear the hologram in half. You still see
The whole landscape, only lower resolution
Only through rain. They call this redundancy
In the literature. It has to do with reference beams
Lines extending to each leaf. As I turned the
They call this contingency, a kind of music
Page I tore it, and now it's elegy
It's autumn. Foils are starting to fall

∝

There are three hundred sixty-two thousand
And that's love. There are flecks of hope
Eight hundred eighty ways to read each stanza
Deep in traditional forms like flaws
Visible when held against the light
I did not walk here all the way from prose
To make corrections in red pencil
I came here tonight to open you up
To interference heard as music

Damaged by flashes, the canvas begins
To enlist the participation of the viewer
To resemble the sitter. Looming sheets
Work mirror flake into the surface
Of curved steel create spaces we can't enter
In that sense is it public sculpture
Beside the office park reflecting pool
I panic my little panic. The death of a
The caesura scales. Autumn tapers

$\propto$

Waking in stations, writing through rain
Which, when it first mixes with exhaust
Smells like jasmine. These are the little
Floating signatures that interest me
Collisions along the path of reference
This time with feeling. What I cannot say is
Is at the vertex. Build your own predicates
In a hand so faint it reads like parting
Out of shifting constellations of debris

I decided to work against my fluency
I was tired of my voice, how it stressed
Its quality as object with transparent darks
This is a recording. This living hand
Reached in error. I hold it toward you
Throw it toward you, measuring the time
Before the waves return from paper walls
Across the lake. Hang up and try again
With poor opacity, with feeling

∝

I decided I would come right out and say it
Into a hollow enclosure producing the
The aural illusion that we are in a canyon
They call this an experience of structure
Or a cave. If it weren't for Ari
In the literature. It has to do with predicates
But it is. I had planned a work of total outrage
Changing phase upon reflection
Until a wave of jasmine interfered

The bird is a little machine for forgetting
The freight trains that pass my house
Every fifteen minutes do not cause any object
In the house to shake except my body
Which makes it seem as if every object
In my house is shaking violently
Is my answer to your question regarding
Content. A better way to put this is
The bird is a little machine

∝

For total war, the memory of jasmine
Paired organs allow us to experience
Contradiction without contradiction
Flowering in winter. Is my answer audible
Or mine, whatever it might mean
Relative to scattering, or am I quoting
The formant frequencies of anchors
What I cannot say. I stand for everything
Like money changing hands in dreams

In the literature. What if I made you
Music that resembles twigs or mimics
Read this as the evolutionary pressure
The meandering lines of the mottled pattern
Obliterate the contours of the soldier
The behavior of a leaf in wind, a feather
To disappear into my surroundings slowly
Infrared is emitted, not reflected. The bodies
Vanish as they cool. They call this crypsis

$$\propto$$

An elaborate allegorization is taking place
In a hollow enclosure as we speak
The question is how to reconcile sleep
An unexpected movement near the face
Cycles with visiting hours. Nocturnal species
Startles me. I nearly wake before regrouping
Yoked together by a common implied verb
To form a flying wedge. Look out
The symbols are collapsing

I'm not above being understood, provided
The periodic motion takes the form of
Work is done on the surface to disturb
Traveling waves. The distances increase
The manmade lake. Metals that behave
In value as the last observer turns away
Like water give us courage to dissolve
And walks out of the frame into
The genre, but not the strength. Wait

∝

I wasn't finished. I was going to say
Into the open, a green place when seen
Through goggles. Virgil wrote at night
From above. Build your own pastoral
Out of embossed symbols, hollow enclosures
Expand on impact in order to disrupt
The Lady of the Lake. A magazine for men
More tissue as they travel through
The genre. We were happy in the cave

I planned a work that could describe itself
Into existence, then back out again
Until description yielded to experience
Yielded an experience of structure
Collapsing under its own weight like
Citable in all its moments: parting
Dusk. Look out the window. Those small
Rain. In a holding pattern over Denver
Collisions clear a path from ground to cloud

∝

Across the lake. I thought that maybe
If there aren't wolves to ring our settlement
It's public sculpture in the sense that
Like everybody else in the gift shop
A refrigerator magnet. Two big bags
I wanted to see what the soldier bought
We could invent some wilderness
Before returning to his dystopic errand
Of mirror flake. A magazine for men

The leaves appear to increase in brightness
The dim star in the periphery disappears
At dusk as rods shift toward the shorter waves
If you turn and try to look at it directly
It maps onto the fovea, rich in cones
Which privilege color over line. I turned
I tore it. Now I see the elegy beneath
Long lines of cloud with poor opacity
A pattern stamped into green foil

$$\propto$$

With feeling, how the eye moves constantly
To keep light from the object falling
Gently on a little clearing. They call this
Like rain that never reaches ground
Reading, like birds that lure predators away
Virga, or the failure of the gaze to reach
By faking injury, like flares that bend
Across the lake in total dark
Missiles from their path

The good news is light is scattered such
Toxicity means the paint must be applied
The apparent brightness of the surface
By robots one atom at a time, bad news
Is the same regardless of the angle of view
I thought I should be the one to tell you
Simultaneously, how monks sing chords
A kind of silence, what we might call
The military applications of Cézanne

∝

Its physics occurred to me while falling
Through rain that wasn't moving. I woke
Before I reached the ground like virga
To find Ari gone. The flattened stems
Only because there was no ground
Allow the words to tremble in the breath
As such. There is no way to read this
Once, and that's love, or aloud, and that's
Breakwaters echo long lines of cloud

Luciferin oxidized by luciferase: night
Writing. They begin to synchronize
Vision green. These are the little floating
Their flashing at the approach of mates
Signatures. Now it is all coming back to me
Or prey. No, I project the false totality
From across the lake in the form of smooth
Reverberant decay. I don't see color
Without tearing off their wings

∝

Is why I'm comfortable with her dream
If you find it maudlin, cut and paste
Of a world without men, but not how you
Is why I cannot touch her with the hand
And another thing: breakwaters echo
A false totality. The goal is to fail
Synchronically, until description yields
Interference rippling across faces
And another thing: the seas

The pitch drops suddenly because the source
Passed away last night in Brooklyn
Hanged himself from the apex in the hope
Left a rent check, a letter in a hand
So faint it read like falling, evening
Of never reaching ground. The siren
The source has stressed his quality as object
Walks through me, opening me up
Recedes. A rain check. This isn't music

$$\propto$$

Sheets of rain create a still space in the city
Where he takes closure into his own hands
We can't enter. This is a holding pattern
This is the lethal suspension of a friend
From a low beam by ligature. Noncoincidence
Of senses, how you feel the train before
You hear the fighter once you've seen it pass
You hear it, indicates a moving frame
Laid to rest is literature

The fovea burns off like fog. A window
Breaks over me in waves. Space is soft clay
Children imply with sparklers, and I find
Sufficient sadness there to organize a canvas
Packed so densely with figures it appears
Let alone a life. The seas are rising
Blank. The seas have long since whelmed
Those cities of the future where my readers
Were displaced. You are free to leave

∝

But not how you mean that, not without
Arising from focusing surfaces charged
Changed in the familiar ways. Little contrasts
With the task of total re-description
To begin the forgetting, a gentle rippling
Across the manmade lake. I planned a work
With appropriate delays, all signals seem
To issue from one speaker. Wait, I wasn't
Continuous in stations, rain

The end. Objects in the dream are sized
He painted what he saw onto the window
According not to distance, but importance
The leaves are falling because his eyes
Because the lines are broken by the breath
Are blank. Questions of accessibility arise
Is lightning. The particles change direction
At funerals. Water spins the other way
Only when I'm asked to read aloud

∝

In a voice so soft it sounds like coughing
Blood into a handkerchief in Russia
The minor novel scales. The weather holds
Forming patterns. I am in Brooklyn
Over Denver, imagining October
Light playing on the body of a friend
Written by Tolstoy. Does that make sense
Or should I describe it with my hands
It's hard not to take the music personally

I know it's full of flowers, music, stars, but
But the pressures under which it fails
How it falls apart if read aloud, or falls
What we might call its physics
Together like applause, a false totality
Scales. The words are just there to confuse
The censors, like mock eyes on the wing
Except for *Ari*. No energy is lost if they collide
The censors inside me, and that's love

$$\propto$$

And that's elegy. I know I am a felt
This is the form where my friend is buried
Effect of the things that I take personally
A gentle rippling across the social body
I know that I can't touch her with the hand
That has touched money, I mean without
Several competing forms of closure
Irony, now warm and capable of
Decay on strings as we descend

DOPPLER ELEGIES

∝

I want to give you, however
            brief, a sense of
period, a major advancement in
I slept through. I want to understand
I want to return to our earlier
I keep a notebook for
            that purpose by
their motion lights, I didn't want
            to wake you, I

sell windows in
            civilian life, I can sleep
anything, the way some people
here, in the terminal
Even as a child, I could sell
look at me, as if to say, what is he
            sleeping, what is Ben
sleeping now. It is as good a word
            as any

war between the forces of
            I wrote this
quickly, over many years
You may have seen me writing it
In photographs, I never know
what they want me to do
            with my hands, I just
smile, but it doesn't mean
            Orange

∞

jumpsuits, they have changed
        painting, I
behind the concertina wire
can't look at it anymore, that wall
across which shadows play
Sorry to be vague
        at such an hour. Were you
When I called, I heard
        my voice

anywhere near waking
        in the background
Strange, reversible lines, I thought
he was dead. He is
better of it, pushing the glass
away. How many songs
        can it hold, that thing
I've seen in windows, has it changed
        singing, or

hooded figures
        I didn't know
it had a camera, some features are
The blue of links, obscure
beneath the face, the green
We still don't have a word for
        Simulated drowning in
embedded streams
        a perfect world

∝

warming, we can enter
          our address, they rotate
slowly overhead, the satellites
I imply their passing when
you're reading, do you think
I wanted it to end
          in complicated paths
like minor planets, flowering trees
          or villages

aflame, please find
          your seat, pretend
to be asleep, then am, head against
the shade, or writing in
a minute hand, yellow masks, unless
Small children traveling alone
          there is a screen
or soldiers, so many dots per inch
          The uniform

becomes you
          Seen from space
it hasn't happened yet, the states
I'm quoting from at night
are red. If they assign storms
proper names, why can't I
          Describe the structure of
feel anything, I mean without
          visuals

∝

built to sway, the saying goes
   Those stars are where
I made some cuts
The last time I saw him was
more or less at random, long
stretches of implied
   flatness, I can't read my own
innumerable tiny marks
   A rustling of tenses

like distant traffic
   overhead, green
zones. On Election Day, make sure
you think of him here
Between commercials, little
glitches occur, so we know it's live
   around the edges, I
organized, distributed fliers like
   This one

goes out to all
   My people were
possible worlds, encouraging
signs, estimated crowds along
the vanishing coast, tonight
is brought to you
   was brought to me
Unfinished, popular songs
   I gathered

∝

quickly, over many years
            Forces are withdrawn
bundled and resold, the words
I distanced myself from
conventional forms, but now
Who am I to say
            at the midpoint of dissolve
I'm sorry, I wasn't listening
            in prose

the weather broke
            When they called
Against the glass, it writes itself
Illuminated prompts
make ordering easy, the way
It's supposed to be a picture of
            flying east, we lost a day
Blank verse returned
            in his later work

To untrained eyes
            it looks like me
Dispersed across regimes, the costs
expressed in human terms
Your machine picked up
the little delays, my intention was
            Occasional
music from a passing car
            for Ari

∝

I'd begin again, this time with
      best practices
Inside the ear, small white buds
At odds with all ideas
of scale, last light glinting off
the wing seen from the ground
      A delicate passage
in a so-so film, from dark to darks
      The real

issue here, in the terminal
      I've come to understand
April can be made into
a thing. I guess that's obvious now
When every surface is
a counter, it's hard to eat
      Among my friends
those paintings double as
      the end

of painting, so this might be
      conceptual
For a while, I thought it was
tentatively titled, a reference to
how waves return
In a cluster of eight poems
      until you let go of the keys
damage is sustained
      Applause

∝

at each mention of his name
          In the long dream
I left it out, that way
We can have the theater to ourselves
across which shadows play
The voice, because it is recorded
          reminds me of
a slow remorse I sampled from
          Yesterday

they were acting strange
          Now they're almost gone
or symbols, which is worse
After the last hive has collapsed
flowers will be poems
Composed entirely of stills
          it doesn't star
anyone you'd know, believe me
          When I say

love, I mean
          and that's rare
enough, low beams exposed
Our permanent achievement
Unbeknownst to us, obscure
forces are at work
          like a radio left on
On the outskirts of
          identical cities

∝

the new construction going up
            is elegy, no
money down or interest through
The twilight of the medium
We're heavily indebted to
interior scenes, now destroyed
            It says so here
On the computer, you can watch
            The seas

are rising, but
            But nothing
anywhere near waking
In the crawl space, we prepared
brief, discontinuous remarks
designed to fall apart
            When read aloud
it reminds me of that time we saw
            silent films

accompanied by
            Her breathing was
a rustling of tenses, underground
Movements have become
citable in all their moments
With my nondominant hand
            I want to give
in a minor key
            the broadest sense

ABOUT THE AUTHOR

Ben Lerner's first book, *The Lichtenberg Figures,* won the Hayden Carruth Award from Copper Canyon Press, was a Lannan Literary Selection, and was named one of 2004's best books of poetry by *Library Journal.* His second book, *Angle of Yaw* (Copper Canyon, 2006), was a finalist for the National Book Award and Northern California Book Award, among other honors. A former Fulbright Scholar in Spain, Lerner teaches at the University of Pittsburgh. He was recently appointed poetry editor of *Critical Quarterly.*

The pressmark for Copper Canyon Press suggests entrance,
connection, and interaction while holding at its center
an attentive, dynamic space for poetry.

Since 1972, Copper Canyon Press has fostered the work of emerging,
established, and world-renowned poets for an expanding audience.
The Press thrives with the generous patronage of readers, writers,
booksellers, librarians, teachers, students, and funders—everyone who
shares the belief that poetry is vital to language and living.

Major funding has been provided by:
Amazon.com
Anonymous
Beroz Ferrell & The Point, LLC
Golden Lasso
Lannan Foundation
National Endowment for the Arts
Cynthia Lovelace Sears and Frank Buxton
Washington State Arts Commission

For information and catalogs:
COPPER CANYON PRESS
Post Office Box 271
Port Townsend, Washington 98368
360-385-4925
www.coppercanyonpress.org

The poems have been typeset in Adobe Garamond, designed by Robert Slimbach for Adobe Systems. Headings are set in Gotham, a sans serif typeface designed by Jonathan Hoefler and Tobias Frere-Jones in 2000. Book design and composition by Phil Kovacevich.

www.ingramcontent.com/pod-product-compliance
Lightning Source LLC
Jackson TN
JSHW052008131224
75386JS00036B/1239